Contents

Fun on a bicycle 4

Helmets 6

Clothes 8

The right size 10

Slowing down and stopping 12

Being seen and heard 14

Cycle paths 16

Crossing roads 18

Staying safe 20

Bicycle safety rules 22

Picture glossary 23

Index 24

Riding a bicycle is fun.

Do you know how to stay safe
on a bicycle?

Never ride a bicycle without
a helmet.

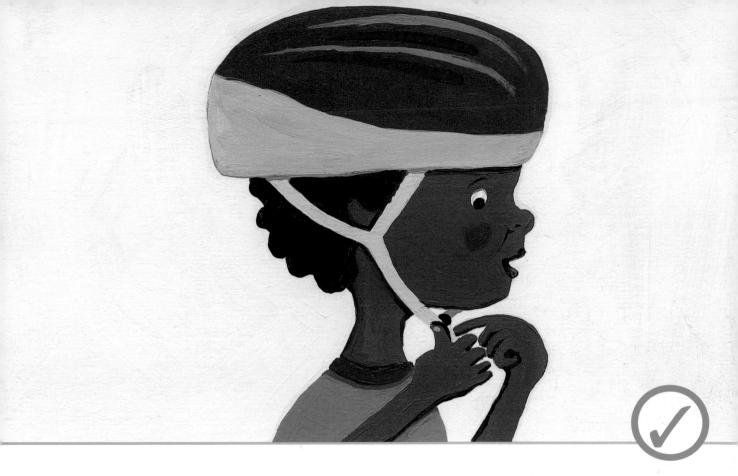

Always make sure your helmet is
on properly.

Never wear loose or baggy clothes on a bicycle.

Always wear clothes that fit well.
Always wear clothes that are bright.

Never ride a bicycle that is too big for you.

Always make sure your feet can touch the ground.

Never go too fast.

12

Always ask a grown-up to make sure your brakes will help you stop.

13

Never ride dangerously.

Always be seen and heard.
Think of others as you go.

Never ride on busy roads.

Always ride on pavements or cycle paths.

Never cycle across a busy road.

Always use a crossing.
Always get off and walk.

Always remember these safety rules.

Always take care on your bicycle and you will stay safe.

Bicycle safety rules

Make sure your helmet is on properly.

Wear clothes that fit well.

Wear clothes that are bright.

Make sure your feet can touch the ground.

Ask a grown-up to make sure your brakes are working.

Always be seen and heard.

Ride on pavements or cycle paths.

Use a crossing to get across a busy road.

Get off and walk when you cross a road.

Picture glossary

 **brakes** parts of the bicycle that make it slow down and stop

 **crossing** place on the road where it is safe to cross. Crossings have special marks or lights.

 **helmet** special hard hat to protect your head

 **path** area that is set aside for people away from traffic. A cycle path is for people on bicycles.

23

Index

brakes   13, 22, 23

clothes   8, 9, 22

crossings   19, 22, 23

cycle paths   17, 22, 23

feet   11, 22

ground   11, 22

grown-ups   13, 22

helmets   6, 7, 22, 23

pavements   17, 22

roads   16, 18

Notes for parents and teachers

Before reading

Show the children a cycle helmet. Ask them what it is. When do they wear one? Why do they wear one? Talk about how strong it is and how it protects their heads.

After reading

Bike map. Draw an outline of a large bicycle onto a sheet of paper and ask the children to help you to label it. Ask them for suggestions as to how to keep safe on a bicycle and write these round the edge of the drawing. Display the diagram for all to see.

Make a helmet. Measure round each child's head and cut a strip of card the correct length. Fold the strip in half. On thin coloured card, draw a circle with a diameter the length of the folded strip plus 3 cm. Fold the circle in half. Attach the straight edges of the half circle round the headband. Leave 3 cm to overlap at the back to represent the shape of the helmet. Wear when role-playing riding a bike.

Bicycle role-play. Encourage the children to role-play riding a bicycle, stopping at the lights, crossing the road, and so on.